This book belongs to...

_____

Once, there was a Hammerhead shark called Mark. Grand in stature, but timid in nature, all Mark the Shark ever wanted to do was fit in.

But the residents of Bubbleton were afraid of Mark. With his great big teeth that glistened like blades in the reflection of the deep blue sea, and his protruding fin that sliced through the water like a hot knife through butter, people in his village knew of Mark... but they avoided him.

One day, as Mark travelled along the sleepy high street of Bubbleton to the usual sound of shop shutters being slammed shut in fear and open shop signs quickly being turned to "Closed" as he passed, a little convenience store caught the attention of one of his widely set eyes.

For outside of this shop, amongst the random selection of brick and brack, sat a lonely little plant pot, with a lonely little root swaying gently in the water's current.

As Mark, the gentle Hammerhead shark, swam over to the store to enquire about this little plant, the terrified shopkeeper, who was cowering behind his tiny little counter yelled, "Just take it, just take it, just don't hurt me!"

Mark, while trying to show the scared little fish that he meant him no harm, flashed him a cheeky smile, but it only made the store attendant more afraid with the sight of his jagged teeth. Off he fled through the streets of Bubbleton, shouting and screaming and warning people of the imminent danger!

Mark was dismayed and hurt but not surprised by the shopkeeper's reaction. He scooped up the lonely little plant pot, left some money for it on the counter, and headed off to his isolated house on the outskirts of the village.

Mark LOVED his new potted companion. He cared for it daily and over the weeks and months that passed, that little root became a small trunk, and that small trunk grew little branches, and those little branches grew tiny little pine needles, and in no time at all, Mark's modest little house, was cast under the shadow of... a huge Christmas tree!

Mark had never celebrated Christmas before as he had never had anyone to celebrate it with. He had been separated from his parents at birth and he had spent his life drifting through the ocean, trying to survive and make friends until he found (and settled) in the sleepy village of Bubbleton.

Mark began to decorate his tree with the brightest coral he could find from the reef. The colours glistened and swayed in the water and provided Mark, the lonely Hammerhead shark, with a warmth that had been missing for nearly all of his life.

The warm glow from the Christmas tree started to grab the attention of the residents of Bubbleton. Murmurs and rumblings echoed through the cobbled high street as people tried to see what the cause of these lights were, all the while trying not to upset the 'dangerous and terrifying' Hammerhead shark that the lights were in the vicinity of.

Eventually, a brave little school of fish, unable to contain their curiosity any longer, decided to swim out to see where these lights were coming from.

As they got closer, their mouths dropped open in awe and amazement at the sight of this beautiful, big, bushy Christmas tree, shimmering proudly in the rippling water. "Hellooooo" rumbled a big bellowing voice from behind the tree. The school of fish scattered, hiding behind the long seagrass and algae, petrified for their lives. "Do you like my tree?" Mark continued... The scared little fish caught a glimpse of one of Mark's separated eyes, peering out from behind his tree. "Do you want to help me decorate it?" He asked longingly, hoping that this may be the chance of some company that he had waited so long for. "My Daddy sells lights in his shop" exclaimed Angus the brave Angel fish. "My Mummy makes glittery bunting out of seaweed" blurted out Tina the timid tuna fish, her fins clasped over her mouth in shock at her own bravery.

"Great!" Said Mark, trying to act cool and not make it too obvious how excited he was about his new found friends, "Let's get to work". Could this really be the first Christmas he wouldn't have to spend alone, Mark wondered?

As word spread through Bubbleton about Mark's Christmas tree, crowds began to make their way (still rather sheepishly) towards the edge of the sleepy village where this lonely Hammerhead shark had been exiled. Coos and gasps pin pricked through the tense atmosphere as they caught their first glimpse of the towering tree, illuminating the hidden depths of the ocean where this scary shark had been residing for all this time.

The schools of young fish darted about, excitedly adding their own prized decorations to the long prickly branches, and cascades of coloured coral draped and shone brightly right to the very tip of the Christmas tree, where Mark was proudly looking down at his glittering masterpiece.

"Hi, I'm Mark" he said nervously to the large gathering, not knowing what type of response he'd receive.... "Hi Mark!" chanted back the fish in excited unison, completely unfazed by him, and more interested in showing their parents their shiny new artwork.

In the years that passed, the decorating of Mark's Christmas tree became an annual event in the village of Bubbleton.

Seeing their young fish getting along so well with this Hammerhead shark that they had feared and revered for so many years, made the parents realise that while they were right to be cautious, they were wrong to judge Mark so hastily and that with a little time, a little effort and a little care, everyone and everything can grow to become the very best version of themselves.

Just like that lonely root, that was sat in a lonely plant pot, that was found by a lonely Hammerhead shark, called Mark.